T0158758

Boundless Awakening
The Heart of Buddhist Meditation

Shamar Rinpoche

Series Bird of Paradise Press

ABOUT BIRD OF PARADISE PRESS

Bird of Paradise Press is a non-profit book publisher based in the United States. The press specializes in Buddhist meditation and philosophy, as well as other topics from Buddhist perspectives including history, ethics, and governance. Its books are distributed worldwide and available in multiple languages. The bird mentioned in the company's name is said to be from a special place where beings can meet with favorable conditions to progress on their path to awakening.

Also by Shamar Rinpoche

BRINGING MIND TRAINING TO LIFE
An Exploration of the 5th Shamarpa's Concise Lojong Manual

THE PATH TO AWAKENING
How Buddhism's Seven Points of Mind Training Can Lead You to a Life of Enlightenment and Happiness

BOUNDLESS WISDOM
A Mahāmudrā Practice Manual

A GOLDEN SWAN IN TURBULENT WATERS
The Life and Times of the Tenth Karmapa Choying Dorje

THE KING OF PRAYERS
A Commentary on the Noble King of Prayers of Excellent Conduct

CREATING A TRANSPARENT DEMOCRACY
A New Model

Boundless Awakening
The Heart of Buddhist Meditation

SHAMAR RINPOCHE

RABSEL
PUBLICATIONS

BIRD OF PARADISE PRESS
Lexington, Virginia, USA
birdofparadisepress.org

RABSEL PUBLICATIONS
16, rue de Babylone
76430 La Remuée, France
www.rabsel.com
contact@rabsel.com

© Rabsel Publications, La Remuée, France, 2020
ISBN 978-2-36017-017-3

CONTENTS

ABOUT THE AUTHOR

Shamar Rinpoche is the 14th Shamarpa. Born in 1952 in Tibet, Shamar Rinpoche was recognized by the 16th Gyalwa Karmapa in 1957, and by the 14th Dalai Lama. In 1996, he started to organize Bodhi Path Buddhist Centers, a network of centers covering many continents, which practice a non-sectarian approach to meditation. In addition, over the years, Shamar Rinpoche has founded several non-profit organizations worldwide engaged in charitable activities such as schooling underprivileged children and promoting animal rights. In a prior book addressing meditation, The Path to Awakening (2009),

Shamar Rinpoche insightfully elucidates Chekawa Yeshe Dorje's Seven Points of Mind Training as both a guide to living a fulfilling life as a Buddhist and a comprehensive manual of meditation techniques.

Whatever arises from the mind,
is of the nature of the mind.
Water and its waves — are they any different?

Mahāsiddha Saraha (India, 8th century A.D.)
Dohakoṣagīti

PREFACE

A first version of this text was published in 1993. It appeared in "Knowledge in Action" the *Journal of the Karmapa International Buddhist Institute* located in New Delhi, India, with Kiki Ekselius and Tina Draszczyk contributing as translators and Mary Parnal as the editor.

This new edition is revised and expanded, and I thank Tina Draszczyk, Rachel Parrish, and David Higgins for their help in editing and proofreading the manuscript. The translations of the quotes from Tibetan were done by Tina Draszczyk.

There is nothing to be removed from [mind as such],
and nothing to be added.

The actual should be seen as actual,
and seeing the actual, you become free

Maitreya/Asaṅga, *Uttaratantra*, I.157

INTRODUCTION

Buddhist meditation is comprised of two aspects: calm abiding and insight. The respective Sanskrit equivalents are *śamatha* and *vipaśyanā*; in Tibetan they are *shiné* and *lhagtong* (Tib. *zhi gnas / lhag mthong*).

The meditation of calm abiding engenders a well-balanced, peaceful, and joyful state of mind. On this basis, the meditation of insight enables us to gain a deep and experience-based knowledge of the true nature of ourselves and of the world of appearances. A main feature of both of these practices is mindfulness, which enables us to fully appreciate the preciousness of each moment of our life.

Before going into the actual topic, I would like to draw your attention to the fact that the limited medium of language is inadequate to convey the actual experience of even the most fundamental forms of meditation and mindfulness. The concepts of any language are based on common experience. Words such as "hot" and "cold," for example, communicate a fairly precise meaning that everyone can agree upon, because everyone has experienced these sensations of heat and cold through direct physical contact at one time or another. This process is different with inner experiences. Inevitably, we are facing a certain dilemma here in that we try to communicate ineffable experiences, such as states of awareness arising in meditation, through language. Therefore, how can we ever be certain that the terms we are applying bring about a certain degree of mutual understanding?

The discussion of philosophical topics is basically confined within the boundaries of shared inner experience, with no external reference point to agree upon. While it is true that over the preceding centuries in languages such as Sanskrit, Pali, Mandarin, and Tibetan a great variety of philosophical Buddhist terms were developed by scholars and meditators, to understand the actual meaning of this terminology requires a substantial background of information and familiar experiences.

I would like to share one example with you to illustrate this point: one key term in Tibetan Buddhism is "ro chig" (Tib. *ro gcig*), which literally translates as "one taste." But what the term means is that, on the basis of true insight into the nature of reality, everything outer and inner is realized in the same manner; this realization, once attained, is unchanging and thus means that all things are perceived evenly or equally. It is one of many levels of accomplishment that can be attained through the practice of "*lan chig kye chor*" (Tib. *lhan cig skyes sbyor*), i.e. the "practice of simultaneity." Obviously, "one taste" is a metaphor for a specific mental experience and does not describe a certain sensation of taste. By means of this term, a person who has experienced the awareness of "one taste" can communicate with someone else who has had the same experience, at least to a certain extent. Yet, for those who don't have this experience, the term most likely remains abstract and difficult to grasp.

This example shows that the respective Buddhist terminology may function as an adequate means of communication between people who share the same experience of meditative insight, but in general, use of it tends to become vague, capable of providing only a rough outline of the intended meaning.

Yet, we do not have many means of communication other than language. Therefore, I will attempt to share my thoughts on Buddhist meditation as well as possible.

My first advice in this context is: begin your meditation in a simple way and proceed gradually to the more advanced levels. Meditative practice in its simplicity is already very profound, and it will become more and more profound as it develops further.

CHAPTER 1: CALM ABIDING MEDITATION

First Steps

The starting point is, therefore, a simple form of meditative practice. In this sense, the first step is calm abiding meditation, a very effective, refreshing, and uncomplicated form of meditation.

Many different methods exist, and all have the same underlying purpose: to enable the mind to remain peacefully and uninterruptedly in a stable state of one-pointed concentration over an extended period of time.

You begin by learning to sit still for periods of

ten, twenty, or thirty minutes, gradually extending the duration of your meditation sessions. The ability to remain in a state of complete absorption is considered to be extremely advanced, but even in the early stages of meditation you can learn to sit quietly and be aware of your mind, observing the flow of arising and passing thoughts that are like the movements of fleeting clouds in a clear sky.

When meditating in this way, paying attention to certain key points regarding the body and the mind is important.

Key points regarding the body: The sitting position

It is best to sit up straight when you meditate. In case you sit on a chair, your feet should touch the ground and be parallel. If you are sitting cross legged on a mat, your legs can be completely crossed in the full lotus position, or alternatively they can be half-crossed with the right leg outside and the left inside. Generally, a person with longer legs sits on a higher cushion, but how high your seat is really depends on your physical proportions. It is important for your spine to be completely straight.

The stomach is slightly drawn inward, while the abdomen is very slightly pushed forward for balance. This keeps the central part of the body very straight. To enhance a straight central torso, your shoulders should also be balanced and straight.

The hands can be placed together in the posture of meditation. This means that the palms of the hands are face up, resting on your heels (if sitting in full lotus position), or resting in your lap a few finger widths below the navel, with the right hand on top of the left. This position further reinforces an upright and straight spine. Alternatively, you can rest your hands face down comfortably on your thighs towards the knees, taking care to keep the shoulders straight.

The neck should be slightly curved so that your chin is a little bit tucked in towards your chest. Your eyes are half open, looking ahead and cast slightly downward. Your mouth should neither be wide open nor pressed firmly closed. The lips should be relaxed in a very natural position. Breathing is mainly through the nose.

These are the essential points of a correct physical posture for meditation.

Key points regarding the mind: How to develop meditative concentration

From among the various techniques we can apply to cultivate calm abiding, the one where breathing serves as a basis for meditative concentration is very suitable. Here there are also a number of possibilities.

You can focus your attention on the coming and going of the breath, simply experiencing breathing in and breathing out. You can also count the cycles of breath if you find it helpful.

Or, you can picture your breath as a bright beam of light. As you inhale and exhale you concentrate on this beam of light flowing through your nostrils. Count each breath—that is, one exhalation and one inhalation—until you reach twenty-one breaths in total. You can start with a gentle inhalation, then start counting from sending out and taking in your breath—one. Out and in—two. Out and in—three, and so forth. Count twenty-one breaths, and then take a short break. Then start again, counting your breaths up to twenty-one, all the while picturing your breath as light.

In the beginning the mind may be distracted, and it will be hard to maintain your focused awareness for the duration of twenty-one breaths. Do not be concerned, even if it is very difficult at first. There is no need to judge your meditation. Whenever your mind wanders around, just keep calmly placing your concentration back on your breath. Counting twenty-one breaths with good meditative concentration will develop tranquility in your body and mind. When you can manage to count twenty-one breaths without any disturbance or distraction, you will already have achieved a very good quality in your meditative concentration. Repeat this sequence of twenty-one breaths, making short breaks of approximately one minute after each cycle of twenty-one breaths. When you can count twenty-one breaths many times with the same quality of meditative concentration, calm abiding in its actual sense can develop.

Stages of progress

At first the meditator's mind is like a wild horse, yet by engaging in the consistent practice of calm abiding meditation it can gradually become tame. Eventually the mind becomes clear and completely free of agitation.

In some instruction texts, the agitation in the mind is first compared to a cascading waterfall, later with the gently flowing currents of a broad river, and finally with the still water of a clear lake on a day without wind.

Outer and inner distractions

In order to lay the foundation for developing the concentrative abilities which are at the heart of calm abiding meditation, we should begin by exploring the nature of distraction to determine what it consists of and how it arises. There are two main categories of distraction: outer and inner.

Outer distraction refers to sense objects in the physical environment such as sounds or visual forms; these sense objects attract our attention almost automatically. Often we are not even aware of being distracted; we don't notice that a sense object has taken our attention, has triggered emotional and conceptual reactions, and has activated certain patterns of acting. In this case we are completely absorbed by the respective sense objects and our reactions, and therefore do not even register how the distraction came about. At first it is difficult to keep the attention from wandering, but slowly, in progressive stages, external distracting influences are overcome. As we become more and more aware of the sensory input, we are alert, and can return to our meditative concentration without delay.

Inner distraction can take many forms, some apparently positive and some negative.

Negative distractions include all types of afflictive mental states, such as anger, jealousy, and fear. Actually, it might seem at first that our meditation practice amplifies our negative thoughts and emotions. This feeling is due to the fact that in ordinary life the mind is usually jumping about here and there in a random, hectic motion, chattering on and on, endlessly preoccupied with one mental activity after another, so that emotional states tend not to be noticed deeply. But in the quiet space of the focused mind, the obsessive strength of emotional and other mental patterns becomes acutely obvious.

Seemingly positive inner distractions involve delightful experiences, and the corresponding distractions are more subtle and deceptive. They have to do with the wonderful, pleasant states of mind resulting from successfully practicing the meditation of calm abiding. They are characterized by a tremendous feeling of contentment, physical comfort, happiness, and well-being, the intensity of which outshines the common enjoyment of sensual pleasures we are used to by far. As such, these pleasant states are perfectly all right. Yet, the difficulty is that the meditator easily becomes attached to them and will strive to bring them about repeatedly. In this way attachment turns these pleasant experiences into a hindrance that forestalls our advancement into further stages of awareness.

How to deal with distraction?

Whether outer or inner, positive or negative, the point is that we have to deal with distractions. As the mind's salient feature is vividness, it naturally moves here and there constantly, and it is also very normal that we become aware of this characteristic in the stillness of meditation.

The training consists precisely of not remaining unaware, of not allowing the distractions to take over, but instead, of registering sensitively and precisely what is happening in the mind, what kind of sensual input, thoughts, emotions, images and so forth are arising and subsiding, without clinging to them.

The nature of meditative concentration

Meditative concentration does not just mean focusing on an object of choice, whether it is the breath or something else. With this type of concentration we will not become aware of the pristine qualities of the mind. Furthermore, after moments of focusing the mind on a given object, it will just return to its usual habit of wandering, as we already know well from our day-to-day life.

Meditative concentration also includes the

awareness of the perceiving mind. The support that helps us to return continuously to the present moment is the object of choice, such as being aware of inhaling and exhaling. Yet, at the same time that you are aware of this support, you are also aware of the awareness. The mind of a practitioner who trains in this type of meditative concentration becomes calmer and calmer, until the focus can be directed entirely on awareness as such. At this point, there is no longer any need for a support.

In this type of "awareness that is aware of itself" meditation, experiences of joy, clarity, and spaciousness—which resembles an all-pervading emptiness—arise spontaneously; these moments of experience are characterized by an absence of ordinary conceptual habits that take phenomena as substantially real and arising from an inherent self-nature. In this context a teacher or guide is indispensable. As we are immersed in the experience, it is difficult to recognize and correctly interpret what is occurring and to deal with it on our own.

Experiences in meditation may have different causes: on the one hand they might be genuine in the above-mentioned sense. On the other hand they might be fabricated by subtle mental inclinations arising from preconceived expectations—merely concepts in the disguise of experiences. A practitioner who is not able to discern this fabrication easily fools himself without even noticing it. Not being able to perceive the subtle workings of mind, we naturally tend to take fascinating feelings and concepts for genuine, uncontrived experiences. Only someone who is familiar with all the stages of meditative practice is able to clearly see what is really going on.

In choosing a teacher, you should understand that the person should be well educated and experienced in meditation, be endowed with a mind of renunciation, patient, and full of care for the student. The teacher should be able to support the student skillfully, without being harsh or discouraging. I cannot overemphasize the importance of finding such a teacher.

Experiences

As we have seen, the arising of an authentic sense of joy, clarity, and emptiness is an indication of successful training in the meditation of calm abiding. When a practitioner is able to handle these experiences without becoming attached to them, he will increase his ability to abide one-pointedly in meditative concentration. And cultivating focused states of mind where the practitioner abides in the direct experience of joy, clarity, and emptiness without judgment and attachment, in turn enhances the quality of the experiences so that they will eventually become stable and lasting.

Experiences of joy—genuine or artificial?

As pointed out above, continuous training in the meditation of calm abiding pacifies the mind which naturally leads to moments of profound, joyful experiences. Yet, good feelings in meditation could also be a kind of invention, a mere projection based on expectation rather than a valid, naturally arisen perception. In the dualistic patterns of our mind we have the habit of searching for something pleasant. We use this pattern as an automatic strategy to counteract uncomfortable feelings or thoughts. In this sense, the mind has the tendency to make up pleasant feelings which we can even take for something real. This type of feeling is just an artificial invention and not a genuine meditative experience.

Experiences of clarity—genuine or artificial?

This mischaracterization is likewise true for the experience of clarity. To counteract our own delusion, which can easily distort short moments of experiencing mind's clarity, we should examine what "clarity" means in this context: the term "clarity" refers to an "awareness that is aware of itself." Sometimes Buddhist scriptures speak about "luminosity," which is a metaphor for mind's vivid, lucid self-awareness. Thus "clarity" or "luminosity" has to do with the capacity of the mind to illuminate itself, to make the unknown known. Again, this language is metaphorical; it is not about light in a physical sense.

In ordinary, everyday life we are usually unaware of mind's self-awareness. Yet, to know itself is an underlying capacity of our mind, which is present in every moment of our life. It is merely due to the constant flow of thoughts, images, and emotions that we are not aware of it. Thoughts and emotions in turn are triggered by the constant physical and mental impulses and processes of sense perceptions. Depending on the respective conditions in the environment—such as light or proximity, and the sharpness of our sense faculties—we perceive a world of appearances and therefore see visual objects, hear sounds, etc. Without being aware of it we act in ways that are conditioned by these stimuli, and are thus in constant interaction with whatever we perceive.

As long as we perceive and experience the various sense objects, but are not self-aware at the same time, we react in a kind of autopilot mode. Such a preoccupied state of mind is actually a kind of stupor or drowsiness, and is based on the ignorance of dense mental states in which self-awareness is lacking. It is an automatically occurring ongoing series of cognitive acts and reactions that take place without our being in touch with the self-reflective, self-aware aspect of our mind. In short, the reflective capacity of the mind that is the basis of wisdom remains inactive. Mental activity that proceeds without our being connected with mind's pervasive self-aware capacity is simply ignorant mental activity. It is a kind of noise that serves to distract mind from its actual nature.

Once training in mindful calm abiding has tamed and pacified the cascade of thoughts, inner images, and emotions, mind's awareness that is aware of itself can emerge on its own accord. In this sense, moments of clarity arise naturally.

Yet, similarly as presented in the context of the experiences of joy, a practitioner might distort genuine moments of clarity as well, trying to create them artificially. This distortion happens when you are attached to short moments of clarity and from then onward yearn to repeat such moments in your mind. Just as with any other impulse we are not aware of, attachment also distracts us from mind's natural self-aware nature. And again we end up in the usual samsaric habit of automatic reactivity.

Experiences of emptiness—genuine or artificial?

What holds true for joy and clarity also applies to experiences of emptiness, which is just another term for the true nature of mind. As mentioned above, in its unaware mode our mind is not aware of itself, not to mention mind's awareness of its actual nature. It is for this reason that everything that surfaces within the mind—thoughts, inner images, and emotions—is taken to be as real and lasting as the seemingly outer world of experiences that we are interacting with constantly.

Once conceptual thoughts, images, emotions, tensions, etc. are pacified, the ground is cleared for moments of experiences of emptiness to take place. However, as was the case with the experiences of joy and clarity, it is imperative that you are not attached to the wish to recreate, prolong, and possess that state. Furthermore, the moments of experiencing emptiness are also mere fleeting experiences. We should not mistake them for the actual realization of emptiness.

Calm abiding—concluding remarks

Practicing calm abiding meditation is the cause for achieving equanimity and peace. Continuous training allows for the experience of a state of calmness in which the mind is capable of a clear focus, being aware of its nature as joy, clarity, and emptiness. For a practitioner who is not attached to these experiences, the gateway for coming into contact with the absolute nature of the mind opens, enabling him to reduce the habit of imposing the mistaken concept of a truly substantial, inherent existence on mind itself.

With continuous practice the potential for these capacities to increase is limitless. It is like a caterpillar emerging from the cocoon as a butterfly. The mind of a person at this level of awareness is totally detached from any worldly concerns or selfish interests, and he is solely concerned with further developing his meditative concentration. However, as great as such meditation states of calm abiding may be, they do not transcend samsaric states of mind, and thus do not bring about ultimate liberation from cyclic existence. They are not comparable to a buddha's awakened state. For someone who wishes to liberate himself from cyclic existence and to benefit others compassionately, the next step is therefore indispensable: the developing of insight.

CHAPTER 2: INSIGHT MEDITATION

Insight, the advanced form of meditation

Insight meditation is the second essential aspect of Buddhist meditation practice. Embedded in calm abiding, insight is cultivated by carefully investigating the nature of the mind and of all appearances. This process opens the access to realizing absolute reality. In the beginning the meditation of insight is thus an analytical process by means of which we look deeply into the nature of reality. The required basis is a calm and clear mind as realized through the meditation of calm abiding as described previously.

At this point I would like to mention that in today's international use of language and in many books on meditation we come across the term *vipassana*, which is the Pali word for the Sanskrit *vipaśyanā*. Its exact meaning varies according to the respective authors and teaching systems. Many make use of this term in a rather general way, relating it to a practice of meditation and mindfulness accessible to beginners.

In accordance with Tibetan Buddhism, however, I employ the term *vipaśyanā* (Tib. *lhagtong*) or insight meditation in this book to refer to an advanced Buddhist meditation practice. In fact, the highest form of sustained insight meditation is simply the perfect awakening of a buddha.

As vipaśyanā consists of the inquiry into the nature of reality, the philosophical schools of Buddhist thought—including the Madhyamaka, which conveys a very profound approach—can be conjoined with this aspect of meditation.

Vipaśyanā or insight meditation is also the core of the practice of the Vajrayāna, specifically of the so-called completion phases (Tib. *rdzogs rim*; Skt. *nishpannakrama*). In general, although they are interrelated, the so-called generation phases (Tib.

bskyed rim; Skt. *utpattikrama*) are rather connected with the meditation of calm abiding. From this perspective as well, it becomes clear that insight meditation is a very advanced form of meditation.

The steps of insight meditation

For the practice of insight meditation or vipaśyanā, a beginner should first of all analyze the present state of mind, understand it, and see in which way it is in a state of delusion. Consistent searching will also inevitably lead us to the causes for this delusion. In this sense, the understanding of cause and effect is also the basis for profound philosophical views.

From the Buddhist point of view, mind is not of a physical nature because it has qualities other than those that are attributed to the brain, which can be viewed and touched. The brain merely serves as a physical substrate for the processes of cognition. The mind as such, however, is not the brain. Yet, mind is not nothing, but is a living experience which is vivid and dynamic. Mind's actual nature is clear, empty, and unobstructed.

If you look carefully into the nature of the mind, of reality, you will come to understand that all outer and inner phenomena, in other words, what seem to be outer sense objects and what appears to be an inner perceiving consciousness, are insubstantial and unreal.

You can start the analytical meditation by first observing the nature of outer phenomena. Then, you continue with observing the perceiver and thus the more subtle processes, the ways in which consciousness perceives and processes everything. This second aspect, which is subtler and therefore less obvious, is the one which is more important in our meditation practice.

Precise analysis will make it evident that the objects of perception that seem to exist as an outer world cannot be anything else but mental projections, appearances known by a mind that perceives its own delusion. Thus, whatever is perceived is an unreal projection that does not exist in its own right, in the way that we usually assume it does. And as there are no outer objects existing as such, the consciousness that seems to perceive them is also understood to be unreal, empty of self-nature. Thus, based on understanding the nature of objects of perception we develop an understanding of the more subtle processes of mind which can furthermore be looked at from two perspectives.

First, a practitioner should become aware of the fact that thoughts and emotions arise and subside in the mind, one following another, in a constant flow of moments with each one distinct from the last. For example: try to count the number of thoughts that occur in sixty seconds and observe how many thoughts, impulses, moments of perception arise and subside during this period of time. You can see that thoughts, perceptions, emotions, and sensations arise and subside, in an ever-changing way. They are not solid entities, and it is not possible to stop their arising and ceasing. You might also try to count the moments in which consciousness takes hold of colors and inner images. Try to find out what actually happens when, by means of the meditation of calm abiding, this constant arising and ceasing of thoughts and images is pacified.

The second perspective consists of observing mind as such, its actual nature, without the various aspects of sense consciousness and the processing of the sense data which always occurs in a dualistic frame. Here we are instead talking about mind itself, the inner experience of self-awareness which does not depend on sensory moments of seeing, hearing, smelling, tasting, touching, and thinking or feeling. "Mind itself" refers to mind free from all of these references. Furthermore, when you turn your mindfulness towards mind as such, thus becoming aware of mind itself, you will discover that all the other moments of perception, from seeing to feeling, will gradually intensify. This process is how heightened sensory perception unfolds.

Dualistic perceptions versus insight

Our present experience, which happens entirely in the context of relative reality, leads us to see the passing mental events—the seemingly outer sense objects and inner phenomena such as perception, thoughts, inner images, emotions and so forth—as substantially real. In fact, their nature is illusory. That is, they resemble images in a dream, changing from moment to moment without any abiding substance to them, yet as long as we cling to their reality, these illusions control us as if they were real.

Once the nature of these mental projections is understood by means of analytical meditation, it is possible to let go of clinging to the seemingly real nature of phenomena. This letting go reverses the habit of ascertaining reality based on what does not have reality in its own right; the pattern of perceiving the world of phenomena, and the perceiving mind, as something real therefore diminishes.

As we realize that neither the objects perceived nor the perceiving mind have a lasting identity on their own, it becomes obvious that they cannot serve as a true ground for a real outer world and a real inner self. Cultivating this insight in meditation makes for the gradual disappearance of confused states of mind and thus leads to transcending cyclic existence—we overcome ordinary states of mind which are governed by delusion.

CHAPTER 3: THE UNION OF CALM ABIDING MEDITATION AND INSIGHT MEDITATION

Having carefully investigated the nature of mind by means of analytical meditation, we thus determine that outer and inner phenomena are insubstantial and unreal. Meditation continues in that we now abide in a calm and clear state of mind with exactly the same insight that was previously achieved intellectually; we settle into knowing the true nature of mind.

Cultivating these states of mind means that we can eventually overcome the tendency of delusion, as mind realizes its own nature more and more. In this sense vipaśyanā, or insight meditation, consists of both analytical steps and cultivating these moments of insight by abiding in them in a calm and clear state of mind. In this way, insight meditation and calm abiding meditation become one practice.

Continuous training therefore allows the practitioner to abide not just in his self-aware mind, but also in the actual nature of the self-aware mind. It is through this approach of meditation that samsaric tendencies, i.e. the artificial dualistic distinctions between an outer world of appearances and an inner perceiving consciousness, will be transcended.

Through the depth of their stability in insight and calm abiding, very advanced practitioners are less and less overpowered by the outer world. Gradually, they are also able to use their perception in order to enhance their practice, and, finally, they are even capable of consciously controlling outer phenomena. A highly accomplished practitioner is thus able to expand the scope and power of his awareness more and more.

The main objective of both the analytical meditation and the calm abiding meditation is to perceive the essence of mind as it truly is. Even a glimpse of this essence is akin to restoring sight to a blind person. Perception of the mind's true nature becomes more and more accurate as the practice becomes more familiar.

To be able to succeed in this spiritual training, it is crucial that a practitioner apply analytical meditation as pointed out above. Even if the first phases of this approach occur on a purely conceptual and intellectual level, this application opens the pathway to an experience-based approach to realizing the true nature of mind. Continuous training will, through the various experiences that occur gradually, allow for a direct insight into reality that is free from conceptualizations.

Everyone who is dedicated in his practice will be able to progress through these various steps of development.

Understanding that the meditation of superior insight that is fully embedded in calm abiding will vanquish all defilements, you must first strive for calm abiding and that is accomplished through the delight in being free from worldly desires.

Śāntideva, *Bodhicaryāvatāra*, VIII.4

CHAPTER 4: THE BENEFIT OF CALM ABIDING MEDITATION

Training in the meditation of calm abiding enables the practitioner to abide in self-awareness. Mindfulness allows for pacifying the agitated and burdening tendencies, thoughts, and emotions. A practitioner, who by means of this training has achieved a certain amount of equanimity and stability and can thus focus one-pointedly without contrived effort, will then be able to investigate these tendencies step by step, whether these are pride, envy, jealousy, anger, fear or others.

As a result, outer objects of focus become inner objects of focus. Instead of holding onto the respective triggers that brought up the various emotions, we are able to analyze the mental processes that occur in ourselves. With this type of mindfulness, the practitioner's capacity to work with afflictive emotions is enhanced. Inner calmness gives him the space to already register negative emotions when they appear in a very subtle way and to let go of them without being overpowered by habitual patterns of reacting.

Furthermore, we become able to understand that thoughts and emotions are but fleeting mental events. In this way, calm abiding meditation smoothes out emotional obstacles in our lives.

Chapter 5: The benefit of insight meditation

The mindful practice of insight meditation goes even deeper: here the actual cause for stress and suffering is analyzed. Precise inquiry into outer and inner phenomena allows for deep experiences of their emptiness. Eventually, as these experiences become stable, the practitioner is no longer overpowered by them; he is aware that all outer and inner occurrences are insubstantial and unreal. Thus, even attachment will subside on its own accord when recognized as empty in nature. This recognition does not, however, mean that the workings of karma in its unceasing flow of cause and effect are discontinued.

Yet, by the time a level of attainment that allows us to truly engage in superior insight meditation is achieved, disturbances relating to karmic effects do not intrude very much.

Very advanced meditators, who have realized mind's empty nature and who are consequently pervaded by compassion for all beings who have not yet realized their true nature, become able to unfold the powers that go along with realization; they are able to use the illusory reality in order to help sentient beings.

Highly realized bodhisattvas who are no longer bound to the concepts of a real world are also able to manifest in different worlds simultaneously, fulfilling the needs of sentient beings.

Buddhas such as the Buddha Amitabha have fully mastered this ability. Thus he, for example, manifests the realm of *Sukhavati* (Tib. *bde ba chen*), while simultaneously manifesting wherever else it is appropriate for him to do so.

CHAPTER 6: LIVING LIFE IN A WAY THAT IS FAVORABLE FOR MEDITATION

Disturbances caused by the karma accrued through non-virtuous deeds and other burdening conditions persist as long as deep levels of insight are not achieved. Therefore, certain recommendations are given in addition to the meditation practice itself.

All in all, it is important that, based on kindness and compassion, we lead a life with an ethical framework that is conducive for meditation practice.

One specific recommendation is to take the vows of a bodhisattva, which entails the far-reaching commitment to subsume our personal desire for awakening under the greater goal of aiding all beings. By making such a commitment now, we sow the seeds for a future development so powerful that our firm and sincere resolve to free all beings from the suffering of samsāra will eventually come true.

It is beneficial to bring to mind that all beings without exception were once upon a time very close and dear to us, because at some time or another during past existences, they have been our fathers and mothers and have shown us immeasurable kindness. Holding this view completely transforms our practice as well, because if the personal motivation of striving for our own liberation is altered through compassion, this alteration is actually the shortest and most direct way of attaining enlightenment. Why? It is because from the very beginning this motivation brings the focus of our thought in line with that of the Buddha.

In taking the vows of a bodhisattva, we promise to follow the guidelines of proper conduct associated with a bodhisattva's lifestyle. Obviously, the vows relate not only to our outer activity, but also to the inner attitude. If the vow is maintained carefully and never allowed to deteriorate, the immense power generated by holding this vow will subdue all kinds of potential emotional and afflictive disturbances and obstacles to our practice. Shantideva, one of the most famous bodhisattva-masters, said in his text, *A Bodhisattva's Way of Life,* "Taking this vow protects you from all types of hindrances."

It is therefore necessary to make continuous efforts to maintain this vow, to inwardly renew it on a regular basis and additionally to become aware of failures. Anger, jealousy, and pride are the main factors that weaken our commitment. Having taken the vows, we should definitely try our best to maintain them, but of course many difficulties will arise, especially in the beginning. It is nearly inevitable that we will engage in mistaken thoughts, words, and actions. As a remedy, it is beneficial to recite Samantabhadra's Aspiration Prayers three times a day while thinking of the welfare of all sentient beings. In this way, the quality of the vow of a bodhisattva will be maintained.

CONCLUDING REMARKS

In conclusion, I would like to encourage everyone to deeply consider the importance of meditation practice. Taking into account the shortness of life it is possible to have a general interest in meditation and to understand the urge of spiritual development. Yet, it is up to everyone individually to really decide that it is truly important for oneself.

Another point to consider is the need for a guide. To ensure a good development on the path we absolutely require guidance and instructions. Relying on an authentic teacher who has trained himself or herself in a reputable Buddhist meditation center, is learned in the skills of meditation, and lives a life of renunciation, will be of great benefit to you.

The sun's nature, bright and brilliant, cannot be dimmed by a thousand eons of darkness, and likewise mind's true nature, clear and luminous, cannot be obscured by eons of cyclic existence.

Mahāsiddha Tilopa (India 11th cent. A.D.),

in *Mahāmudropadeśa*

Publishing finished
in February 2020 by Pulsio
Publisher Number : 4007
Legal Deposit : February 2020
Printed in Bulgaria